AWAKE

POEMS ON TRANSCENDENCE

SILVIA MARIA PORRO

BALBOA.
PRESS

A DIVISION OF HAY HOUSE

Balboa Press books may be ordered through booksellers or by contacting:

Balboa Press
A Division of Hay House
1663 Liberty Drive
Bloomington, IN 47403
www.balboapress.com
1 (877) 407-4847

Print information available on the last page.

ISBN: 978-1-5043-4548-4 (sc)
ISBN: 978-1-5043-4549-1 (e)

Balboa Press rev. date: 1/18/2016

Table of contents

Introduction   ix
Chapter One – Sleep   1
Chapter One – Sleep- Table of contents   2
Extinct   3
Ninth Sleep   4
The Blue   5
Moon Roving   6
Waiting   7
A game you played   8
S.O.S.   9
Each Day   10
Absence   11
No Comfort   12
Brick House   13
The Noon Day Sun   14
A Poem for my parents   15
The Grandest landmass   16
Feeling You   18
His house on the hill   19
Chapter Two – Rebirth   21
Chapter Two- Rebirth- Table of contents   22
Ascent of the Gods   23
LionHeart   25
Still   26
Freedom   27
Traveler of space and time   28
Breathe   29
That small door   30
Power of Grace   31
To The Dawn   32
Where you stand   33
Fly   34
The Poem is You   35
My Heart Tells me That.........   37
I Am   39
One   40
And we dance our endless dance   41
Twin flames   42
Awake   44
About the Author   45

For my beloved mother, Silvia Orquidea Quiñones Porro.

You have shaped my life, forever.

One day, we will be together, again.

"Awake" is a collection of poems expressive of a timeless life; in sleep, transcendence and wakefulness. It is a personal journey, honoring of life, connection, reciprocity, truth and evolution, inherent in all of us. I began this writing, at a time of deep transition, in my life. Within the pages of this book lie an expression, integration and transcendence; a living, breathing chronicle. Its unifying story is shaped by the greatest catalyst for my spiritual development; my mother.

The verse in "Awake" accedes pain and loss, in layers of consciousness and change. Thus, it is not exclusive, in its definition. The life force that carries its message travels across species and opens with "Extinct"; an ode to the largest Earth-dwelling mammal whose inter-relation with the human race carries the potentially fatal hazard of its abrogation. As such, this expression becomes its voice as well as a calling to the highest human consciousness; that which carries a knowing of the inter-relation of all living organisms. "Extinct" is the first poem of the first chapter, entitled "Sleep." It shines a light at the unconscious nature of a yet unrealized, destructive action that is, at once, in human hands, inhumane.

This awareness is also called upon through the poem entitled "Waiting." "Waiting" reflects a depiction of human indifference toward an extraordinary canine fidelity. Its social meaning reflects a discarding of an earnest life, symbolizing a false superiority. It bears witness to the fate and irony of many animal harborages, in today's society that cut healthy lives short.

"The Blue" depicts the need for human consciousness to awake to the endangered existence of the largest breathing animal to inhabit the Earth's oceans; The Blue Whale. Their numbers are endangered due to whaling, entanglement in long-line fishing gear, ship strikes, military sonar & weapons testing exercises, oil spills and climate change. It is in a literal, actual sense, the greatest call to life as it is, at once, potentially, the greatest blindness. In our inter-relation with animal species sharing our blue planet, human consciousness is marked both by action and its inaction.

"LionHeart" depicts the transforming power of courage-an unrestricted part of the whole. I have integrated the theme of a collective consciousness in my work, over the years-both in paintings and the written word. For me, there is little else more reflective of our transcendence and evolution than our ability to connect with a living consciousness and step out of ourselves to see that connection and bridge the gap between us. This gap is where the greatest consciousness resides; the seeds of evolution. We must acknowledge the life that flows through all of us if we are to prevent its extinction.

Within the pages of this book lies the knowledge that deconstruction is a part of the change that precedes its transcendence. Also present, in this work is a vestibule of layers of sub-consciousness, consciousness and a deeper consciousness that may be interpreted as a transcendental shedding of the physical skin. It is an expression of an evolving non-physical consciousness. This living process may be internalized through the reader's interpretation of "Ninth Sleep", "Traveler of Space and Time" and "Moon Roving."

"A poem for my parents," "The grandest landmass," and "His house on the hill" pay homage to my family and my Cuban-American heritage. Chapter two is entitled "Rebirth." It carries poems expressing a rebirth of life, transcendent love and joy. It carries moments filled with connections; the dance and fluidity of an awake life. "Each day, "S.O.S." and "Power of Grace" give voice to social consciousness, the oppressed and their inherent liberation.

"Each day" and "Power of Grace" honor the extraordinary power, love and courage of women; that which is revealed through a disarming, subtle, inter-generational sexism and transformed through the evolution of Grace (the "Power of Grace.")

"Each day" gives voice to the evolution of human consciousness by raising awareness surrounding the Humanitarian infallibility that supports the civil rights of life partners, regardless of gender. This book strives to express a liberation from labels, concepts and judgments that blur a reciprocity with a collective consciousness; a union with The Divine. "Each day" bears witness to a dismissed, powerful love; that which sheds light on the invisible, thereby making it, visible. It illustrates a social denial that is alienating, in the face of loss.

"S.O.S." is a call for the liberation of citizens who exist under the rule of oppressive governments and show unimaginable courage, for the liberation of their countries and the restoration of their lives. It is one voice, for countless who have lost their lives, as they fight for the freedom to live.

"Ascent of the Gods" elucidates a sacred communing with the Redwood trees that live in the forest of Muir woods, on the coast of Northern California. It shares a personal journey; bathed, centered and transformed by what may only be succinctly described as the presence and breath of God.

The ancient inhabitance and requited inspiration towers over me, in sublime awareness, still………

I feel whole, supported, protected by a guiding spirit. In those moments, I live continually, in a sustaining wisdom. This poem honors this spirit by bearing witness to an omnipresent sentience, as well as the transcendence of a lower-level consciousness. This lower-level consciousness endangers the Earth as well as environmentalists protecting it. Its peril lies in the deforestation and pollution that fronts global warming. These environmentalists and investigating reporters are endangered and threatened through pecuniary manipulation (the carrot) and physical threat (the stick). The origin of this contrasting consciousness involves commercialism, upheld, through the destruction of the Earth's natural resources. It describes one perspective surrounding the process of finding one's deepest identity, uniting with Nature, in our journeys through the Earth, in this life span.

As such, this verse is an awakening to prevent the destruction of the planet we inhabit, and its surrounding atmosphere.

"Awake," the last poem of the series, depicts a deep calling to transcend a progressive, powerful disease, over a span of a lifetime, on an intra-personal and inter-personal level. It acknowledges this potentiality, in all of us, in our human experience. It calls for its perseverance and knowing; that of the evolution of a transforming, healing empowerment. It speaks to the power of the human spirit to transcend disease. Again, it is within the reader's discernment that she/he may relate their world to come to these written words. The underlying energy that carries the message that is "Awake" is a collective consciousness that is its vehicle. As such, it is my hope that this body of work may be a means to awaken, in the reader, an evolution of her/his deepest realizations.

The cover photo of "Awake"; a human eye, denotes a deep reflection and awake state that is, hopefully, enduring, revealing and transforming. It is a connection; a revival that opens a conscious life.

Every being I have loved lives in these pages. I consider it a great privilege to be able to express a piece of their lives, as they have united with mine. I am very grateful for all those beautiful, beloved beings who co-created this living chronicle with me. I have gained lifetimes of wisdom through the Grace of your presence, in my life. Thank You.

Silvia Maria Porro
Miami, Florida
Spring 2015

1

SLEEP

*"Each night, when I go to sleep, I die
And the next morning when
I wake up
I am Reborn." –Mahatma Gandhi*

*"The wound is the place where
The light enters you."-Rumi*

1

Extinct
Ninth Sleep
The Blue
Moon Roving
Waiting
A game you played
S.O.S.
Each Day
Absence
No Comfort
Brick House
The Noon Day Sun
A Poem for my parents
The Grandest landmass
Feeling You
His house on the hill
Ascent of the Gods

Extinct

Extinct
In blindness
My charge crumbled
At your small, dark hands

My species cries its decimation
Camouflaged

Unfathomable

Lost in my memory
And the grief of a thousand offspring

A veritable mammalian
The greatest in Girth and Eminence
To ever walk the Earth

Without Attrition
To meet
An unmeasured sapience
Through weathered, leathery skin
And old eyes

An ardent herd
Humanity may never rise to

Lying in a jarring stupor
Draped by the trunks
Of an Elephantine
Occlusion

In denying me
You deny you

How will you Awake
At Dawn?

Ninth Sleep

My greatest bliss lies in your silky, liquid pools
As peace enters me and gently enfolds my every cell

I return to selfless oceans of oneness

And shed my skin

An effortless vestibule of consciousness drapes me

All travelers hold my every fiber
A oneness of being travels through me
Extending my consciousness
In liquid, light-filled presence

I am free

My life flows through me
Caressing me, in its Prana

Universal energy elevates my senses
In my Ninth sleep

And I awaken.......to see
What my physical eyes could not fathom.........in one lifetime

The vastitude
Of your rapture

The Blue

The largest, breathing energy
A continuance
A covenant
Life

Through deep, dark oceans
Aqueous, in their massive balance
Carried, by their flow

The Blue pulses its existence
To hear its own   one thousand miles deep
A life span   one hundred years long

A pod of Blue Grace
Its cries penetrate The earth's core

Unheard by its kill
Entangled in blindness
Struck by weakness
Transformed by its climate
Dismissed by a ravenous callowness

Its Blue-gray magnificence
Flying, in the deepest body of water
The darkest chasm

Deafened by outcry
Endangered by indifference
A detonated silence
Destroyed in fear

A testament
A knowing
The greatest veneration   to Life

Moon Roving

Your velvety, soft cocoon gently guides my senses
To your luminosity
In black perfection
A million eyes of light, gaze at me   completing me

My exhalations bring me to my exhilarated body
Its blood, pumping its thirst for knowledge

With my heart in my throat my lungs e x p a n d with awe

Enveloped in your bliss
I land my Eagle, in your tranquil sea
My eyes are flooded with rich vessels
Staring at overwhelming visions of v a s t ,   g r a y ,   p u r i t y
They may not see, in one lifetime
Yet, I have, somehow
Your craters invite my abandon and total submission
This moment in time- **mine**
Let me whip across your atmosphere!
At peace with the Universe
In a oneness of time

Waiting

You cannot
See
The layers of truth
In my eyes

In my presence

You occlude my species

Deny my soul

Forget my l o n g e s t memory

But I have always known

And walked
A million mile path
Of rocky roads

My pads, stained
With the loyal blood that courses through
My veins

To your absence
And stayed there
For an eternity

A game you played

I was young
when my rolling laugh
left my tongue

and disappeared
in the mist
of the morning

and my bald head
concentrated its mind power

on golden books
and apples

and my life
rolled down the hill
with you

and I thought
it was

A game you played

S.O.S.

One more walk, under a heavy sky

Miles to cross
With bleeding hearts
To straighten an oppressed gait

To feed a hunger
To find my life, in the dark
To fight for humanity, with my last breath
To right a wrong
To live with myself

A thousand dulling senses never forget
A freedom cry, to the head!

A student of life
A child of mine
Raises his voice to change the tide

Lies, crimson, in its wake

Only Human

My country!
My Mountains!
My Blood!
My Fall!

The Earth grounds my identity

A sea of blistered hope
A solidarity of unknown strength

A blindness stirs the endless fire
A release drives my charge

Humanity disperses
Once more, to the streets!
To lose ourselves
In the wind

Each Day

My eyes dimmed
Like a hollow caved in

With the sound   of your absence
T h a t   c r u s h e d   m y   c h e s t

My touchstone!
My beam!

Bracing myself for high tide
That had waned, with the world
In the presence, of your smile

Now   Gone

Sharpness shoots up and down my skin
Unprotected, by your touch

I stand stark

Numb, to empty minds
And fearful stabs

In the dark

F
  A
    L
      L
        E
          N

from bliss, out of a net hold
of an invisible life

to those who fail to embrace Love

Each Day

Absence

What drags my days and trailing gravamen?
What force changes the tide?
What strengthens my motion to climb?

A surreal puzzle challenging a fragmented mind?

Dug down, deep in my boots
In the pouring rain that failed to wet my dulling senses
Wide-eyed now, with pain
This is a less passionate journey
But one and the same

From other maps, expanded and revised
An uncommon valor
Strength of time and laborious mass

A solid leap of faith

And now, I must deal with your

Absence

No Comfort

Unused to kindness   Open my mind
My skin craves truth   A rain of light

My voice, fragmented in pain
Soothed by your song   held, in your elusive arms

Traveled through lifetimes   to this emergence

My body; a vessel, unversed in its core
Immeasurable in focus   Now

What is the depth of your pain?
The meaning of your life?
Your Eternal Breath?

The weight of my deepest anguish   carried forward
The whole of my life   collected marrow
A fragile distress   through chasms of doubt
The distance of the world

Lost in its tumultuous wave
Again and Again

Wordless
Breathless
To surface my aching tenement
And gasp at the deep sky

I meet you there
A knowing
Its deepest cause steadies me   as its ardor struggles to break free
Jumps from my hands   with its beating heart

To Live Again

Brick House

The steel beams weigh on each step you take
Down the street

Intruding your mind   that doesn't see
The floating birds   up the shafts of light

To spills of generous latitude, amplitude and risk

The friction of your collar tugs at your unknowing body
In its routine, awaiting a roar of excitement to feed it

As you walk, down the street to lively sounds
In windowed rows, that clog your brain
With inviting fingers that numb you

At each corner, foreign laughs square off; exclusive, in their pain
But you are not mad, simply analytical and ruminative
In your space; a walking house of brick.........

Throw the keys down the street!
See if you miss or learn a new trick
Play with your hands   await your chance   and walk again
The endless endless endless walk

Who built this house, so heavy on my mind?

So hard to knock down
One brick, at a time

The Noon Day Sun

I turn the page with a new hand   callused and strong
Preparing to dip into the deepest breach
To find myself there

Wading, on the surface
The diver lost its bulk
Washed away with the tide, and a new course

I remember your livelihood
In more than one form
My arms will have to grow now
Across space and jagged time
As long as the days
As deep as my mind
That reached for your senses

That I may taste warmth

The Noon Day Sun

Blisters my skin

And I lay

Undone

A Poem for my parents

Tough, yellowed scrap papers bring a twinge of longing to know about you
Like an ache, at my side moving me, to apprehend my loves
As they fade.........

While your crisp beauty luxuriates my senses
Shiny pools, with trails of light on trees of old filled trunks of hope

While your tough boy's attitude leaned on the wasted cement wall

And her mind.........

And the checkered linoleum held her model's masculine stance
Next to the antique typewriter

While you weaved between palm trees; woozy in your love
And every blade of grass was new

The distant beauty of blue waves, plum crests and green eminence
Embraced you

Smiling, on chipped boulders
The powder-blue El Dorado, shining
Beyond the swaying pine
Beckoning your escape

Your silhouettes softened the jagged, gray cave
With draping vines

And pure lives were shaped
As I was deliberately waiting
Maybe, for a dream

The Grandest landmass

The grandest landmass
like a grandparents' tale
or a parent's dream
of children playing
by a stream

Is not the same to me

When I see children run, and throw balls
At structured walls
Unbeknownst to their power

With innocent, dancing eyes
Running, in old shoes as if their feet were out of place

In the enormous emptiness
The Historic gates surround them

Barely surviving the test of time

And I have played on those palace steps
Or farmlands of oceans of palm trees, in far-off provinces

To breathe life into them, if I knew how

Like an old man, in love with his land

As your handkerchief face peeks out the windowed row
At the corner of 154
With clothesline vision, hoping for a mischievous distraction
To your drooping jaw

Your once grand buildings are wasted, with dimming lives inside
Awaiting their renovations, they cry
Leaking, air conditioned tears, in the heat

Next time we meet, lost in your deep harbor

I look at your soul, for the first and last time

At the center store, with yellowing photographs,
Yearning old time
Past the prickly pear valley and 50's vintage autos of yellow,
Blue and red, that bring the only color I see

And some dread

To clusters of shrubbery, I see, from the top
Peeking out from miles of pink concrete, orange tile roofs
And domed fortresses

I try to understand

Down the steps, finding an inch of comfort
In your snug and narrow, cobblestone streets

To my heart of hearts!
At home in another lifetime
As my green, marble wings fly me off their concrete perch
To your vast sovereignty
Dancing with the clouds
At last

Feeling You

So Close
In your skin

I feel you

Once removed

Fill me with substance

Boundless
Spirit pulsates through my body

Your vibration enters me,
holds my hands, leaves my fingers

Energy pulsates through my inmost being

A Higher Love enters my chest

Opens me

My Awareness
A blue sky

In my face
Unveil your fear
It is One
And I
Hold your heart

My eyes
Watered down
In a life span
Meet your steady form

A patient warmth
Certain, in its decree
To Rise

His house on the hill

His stocky, weathered frame is held up by his walking stick
His rancher's hat spies a land of bittersweet remembrance
And resigned faith

Like pure water
In his rough and gentle hands
That have cut a thousand canes
And steadied a worried child
There, he heals.........

His house on the hill is discolored, now
The paint is peeling

He lived in that yesterday, once

I listened, warmly to his anecdotes
And romantic, Cuban ballads
He didn't need anything, then
He was a quiet fighter
A boxer.........
Accompanied by his lady, on the balcony

Now, he colors
Orange bunnies, turquoise birds, blue-eyed daisies
And his tri-colored house on the hill
To give to me, my child

There, he heals

REBIRTH

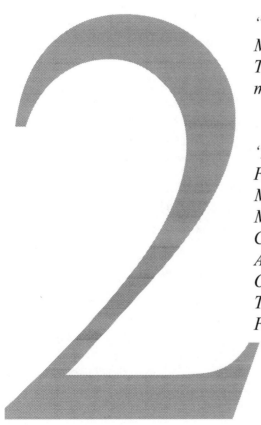

"With my ninth mind, I resurrect
My first and dance slow to
The music of my soul
made new." – Abajhani

"Awake, shake dreams
From your hair
My pretty child,
My sweet one.
Choose the day
And choose the sign
Of your day
The day's Divinity
First thing you see" – The Doors

LionHeart
Still
Freedom
Traveler of space and time
Breathe
That small door
Power of Grace
To The Dawn
Where you stand
Fly
The Poem is You
My Heart Tells me That.........
I Am
One
And we dance our endless dance
Twin flames
Awake

Ascent of the Gods

An ancient presence holds me
In the light

A pervading longevity
Deeper
Higher

Than an unsettled apperception
Moves a carrot and a stick

Outlives senescence
Resplendent
Omnipresent
Majestic in its Power

The center of my past
My presence.........Endless

A Sacred grove
In high altitude
Bathes my meridian
In the mist of the morning

Bestows energy to live

The breath of its scale

A witness
To the core

A warming planet
Outside,
A
Cold
Mind

The Earth's silentious sentinel

A green gas
Consumes its mass

Penetrates evolution

Aboriginal Giants
Rise, as Titans
In the Day
And the Night

Watchers of time
Tenacious
In depths

Knowing

Vibrate
Your
Auspicious
Being

Silently skinned

An aura ascends
Aloft
The base

A human fog

Address the Eternal

LionHeart

A guttural stirring
Burns at my core

To shelter the pack   to the Death

A choked erudition
An animal instinct

To die   to live   Every Life

My territory embraces my birthright
Lurking, in the Night

It lunges with the courage of my ancestors
Born, in the dawn

I circle the plain that marks my existence
The Horizon charges   at my arch
With its blinding light

And I see

The sun burns its permanence   to my core
The wind carries my identity

My heart fills a dauntless, endless tread

TO BE FREE

Still

Your presence holds me, in its entirety
Your sapience permeates my existence

Your taste inhabits my being
Your aura enters my body

In
Your
Transforming
Spirit

I
Lay
Still

Freedom

Across time and space

I reach you

A certainty fills

My infinite space

Channels bridge endless colors

Of light and creation, that soothe my wounds

And open my spirit

Beautiful, to the core

I spread my wings to fly

Your decorated body glides through me

Changing me

And I know

Traveler of space and time

I have traveled, for lifetimes now
From the greatest peak   I breathe in the ethereal clouds

In intoxicating laughter   I am held by your hand
The nethermost space; I inhabit

A swell of Divine presence fills my vessel

An aura of peace has always risen, after the storm
To an open spirit

My body loses its mass, in its intense devotion
We nurture an unexpected elevation

Our bodies burn with every fiber of light that has ever lived

And we come together
As we always
Have been

To lift ourselves
From a big sleep

Breathe

My undulating pulse steadies its strength
Striding now

Persistent throes carry me
My whole skin craves its amenities

Long years rest on your chest
Wounds heal in your arms
Doubtful lines erased by your fingers

Hopeful breaths wrapped by your gentle, guiding limbs
Float, effortlessly into space

Balanced, on my laurels
Wordless light attunes your meaning

Knowledge seeps into your being

My spirit flies, safe in your harbor

Where I Breathe

That small door

Once in a life it holds your grip

And   o p e n s   your mind

And summons the wind of time

Power of Grace

Subtle words drape over my shoulders
Disguised as silk

Womanish
In your discernment

Identities
Handed down
From generations past

Dismissing the greatest seed

Bear witness to your dulling voice
As if it were
Mine

And I come
To my senses

Grace disarms your innermost power
And gives birth to your Old Soul

A verity inside
Long denied

The greatest sex
In deference

A free voice
Intones the blue expanse

At once
Meeting
Your light

I Am

To The Dawn

I follow my inner light
Anxiously.................
Pounding.................

My heart, my legs, so full, in deliberation
A rented space of rumination

In steady, stomping beats
Fighter of timeless feats

Finding minds and gathering arms, along the path
That had lost their footing

With chaste vigor, in my veins
An unobtrusive pain drives my tremulous charge

To The Dawn   where I am found
Where others see, with new eyes and think in wavelengths

The Dawn, where fresh tastes melt on our tongues
Forming novel cerebration   expressed in oneness

Where I can breathe, again
In heaves and enduring beads
That seep through my potent marrow

The Dawn, undulated and refined
In my burdened mind

To open my soul

To hold you again

Where I am released

Where you stand

One thousand anguished screams seeped through my pores
sprawled from the summit   it dips to my soul   where I stand

to greet a new era   with an empty plate
and camouflaged spins and yowls

making my way through yore, dimmed in the night

to a brotherhood in arms   my hand- a camera
its viewfinder, dazed in the moment

as towers chime   for all time

energize my elusive countenance!
dress it well to bear witness to this time!

full of burbling masses, rising as mist, over the city of lights
with fire-crackling explosions of oneness
up and down iron shafts, in exultation!

Outward!- Shooting vast sparks of golden spears
Beaming and beautified, down to your core   where you stand

Blessed, without cause   intone your voice to the Heavens
consumed by its luminosity   ever-glowing in its harmony

as midnight's global progression overwhelms a century
of spilled desire, rotating vision and gathered hope

And we perform to creation   This is our moment to shine!
our boats parade our harbors   lining a serene sea
so we can take the wheel   to re-write our actuality

Re- enact again and again!

Scrub your soul to the end!

Arise, my friend

For I may not find you among the strangers I bosom

and your empty calls won't fill me

as my deluge falls, silent to your ears

Fly

Fly   My   love
Fly   your tears
Fly your feelings

Fly with the wind that gives you breath

That which moves the Heavens and Earth

Fly with the joy that has always been..........

In the freedom of that encounter

Fly forever.........

The Poem is You

With an Elevated Spirit
An Integrated Divinity
In the Power of Now

You are The Mountain
Alpine, Strong and clear in the morning
You yearn the ice that melts your doubt
You breathe the life that lifts my levels of consciousness

You are the birds
Without a Name, in Free Flight
Without knowing how or when
In the center of your identity and Grace
Accepting the Air, The Elements
Life, E n d l e s s
Never before seen
You feel my ascension as you fly, in a nurturing certainty
Over a fascinating body of water that flows, nude
In the current of change
With the depths of its mysterious and seductive waves
Reflected, in me

You are the Ocean   deepening in its fluidity
The current that unites us
Cleaning the consciousness of provoking storms,
Transcendental and Ethereal
Where the light enters, illuminates and lives
In the veracity of your being
The Medulla of your existence
You bathe and strengthen my fragility
With life-giving breath   you murmur my Rebirth

On the dark side, your Faith grows
With lucidity, you give yourself to the Night
With one strong and brilliant point of light
You appear and disappear, as a guide through the Darkness
I am pliable, in your Presence
Your inspiration moves me and I lose my breath
For a moment

You are The Stars
With hands of hope
With fingers of illumination
You reach in me, what slept for a lifetime

And now words leave
They disperse with the perspiration of
The Unknown
And you Dance to Honor Me
With Full Eyes
With your deepest Spirit
Hands trembling with Emotion
Those that awake in me
Those I have always waited for
And never imagined
Danced for Me

My Heart Tells me That.........

My Heart tells me that.........
I have danced with pain
For half a century now.........
Its mark creates a form, I enter
Unrecognizable, to the naked eye

My Heart tells me that.........
I have danced with a boulder on my chest
An empty space created by an inexplicable absence

My Human question awaits the center of Truth;
Transcendent, Evasive

My Heart tell me that.........
I am lost
And my walk refines my nucleus
But I am deaf; Half a century; a lifetime, for many

My Heart tells me to confide
But I am mute; Half a century; a lifetime, for many

I am surrounded by gray veils
Silent
To Re-awaken Acceptance
De-constructed, Reborn

There, in the emptiness
We all look to the Horizon
To savor its juicy delicacies
That coat my window

To inhabit her sigh
To inhale her sweet aroma
To caress her skin with fingers of milk and honey
Creating a United lucidity
To hold a heart with another, as it palpates its truth
To lift aspirations to the wind
Inebriated with life

My Heart tells me I am dancing with love
Mischievous and Alive
Wet and enveloping
Courageous and vulnerable
Tender to the touch
And, with its tenderness
Discovers my being
In the ecstasy of its re-awakening

My Heart tells me its fluidity integrates its message
Now
An Eternity
In one drop of water- An Ocean

My Heart tells me
It is dancing with my Spirit
Opened by the light of a million Suns
In pure flight
In the freedom of transcendence
Where we elevate
Very far from concepts, ideas, time, moments

The Divine tells me
I Am

I Am

I Am here and Now
Without a history

Without a way
Without a defining pain

I Am the rain
Washing over you

Your soul
Embracing

Awakening your skin
Sunlight

Endless Presence

I Am

One

The warmth of your Spirit calls me
In its Elegance

Fibrous hands hold my breath across a room
Illuminated by your beacon

An invisible thread

Destined to meet

My gaze caresses your skin as I enter your dance

Fear lost
Many lifetimes, past

Free from our vessels in timeless space

The motion of our lives fills my marrow
My eyes dance, with anticipation
From a precipice, I fall to you

And the fluid vastness returns
Lifting and caressing us

The Universe enters us
Holds us
In its knowing

Your longing moves me to live and die once more
To shed my skin

And you, with your Grace
Lift my spirit

We are Light
Particles flowing softly through space
To ascend
As
One

And we dance our endless dance

I am a path to you, for lifetimes   until now, unknown
Every breath labors, with an unseen strength that pulsates its truth
From the occult

With steel arms and legs   to carry my compensated truth
To your eyes

We are mirrors without judgment
Fluid spirits rise from ethereal oceans
To rest
In each other's arms

An ascendant essence   Majestic   Pure
To Encounter Love there

Raw, from its tether
Ripe with the strength of a runner   now seeking rest

Leveled by the path of a hunter   whose vessels carry a certain truth

A growing presence, formed and caressed
By an abiding Grace
Light arises from darkness

Your luminous essence rises from our center
Rays of light, in your eyes

Discovering our truths

An astounding presence   too brilliant to see
And we dance our endless dance

Twin flames

My insides long
to be held by your conscience

A spark
leaves a   t r a i l
of you
smoldering, in my senses

an endless span
traverses through
the entirety of two lives

flows through
every rumination
as a bee   dances with a tulip
darts across the night

dims my marrow

slightly above my reach
I still see your beauty
In my mind's eye
I am holding you

dispersing time
turns white

screams its truth
in the dark

deaf to your ears

an elusive flow
water through my hands

I run to you

slip in devotion

empathetic
mindful
a dimming hope
in your silence

vacant footsteps
meet
an uninvited vicissitude

for an instant
your travels become mine

I willingly enter your flow

the darkness
and the light

recessed spaces
of your brilliant mind

shine
and
dim
with the flip of a switch

in your absence

your silence meets mine
as if we never met

evading
a
Higher
expression

fearful of the light

it has embodied
for lifetimes   now

Awake

A warm surge
Fills the back of my neck
Your energy fills my vacant life
Driving an unforeseen path

Disguised as pain
To strengthen my form
Unbeknownst to me

A taker of lives
Meets my gait
From a distance

A calling

To dive to the depths
Of your existence
To find me there

A seducer of time and space
A thief who has stolen everything

Knees hit the gravel
A cold, blue form
Reached the sky, then digs deep

The Earth hears a feint heartbeat
It is not done

A taker of lives
Takes truth
Wrapped in lies
Collects identities
To a deep void
Blurs the connection to

The Divine

Until I

Awake

About the Author

Silvia Maria Porro is a Licensed Mental Health, Drug/Alcohol Addiction Therapist, Artist, Writer and Poet living in Miami, Florida. She has worked in the Behavioral Health Services field for twenty seven years. Her experience in the behavioral Health service field, as well as her personal experience has enabled her to intuitively embrace a living truth, in the knowledge of its healing, empowering, freeing and transcendent power through several different processes. All evoke beauty in transition and being. Her ever-growing body of work strives to connect to human/animal consciousness in order to connect to an innate free nature and transcend pain and suffering. This work sheds light on our living collective consciousness. Her work conveys, most of all that Art and the power of Spiritual practice are inseparable and infinite.

Art exhibits she has participated in, to-date, include a group art show in Coconut Grove, Florida to save the bees. Her Artist website is: **Sporro999.wix.com/spirit-studio** and Poetry website is: **sporro999.wix.com/awakepoems999**

Her facebook Artist's page **is** Spirit Studio/Silvia Porro